Marvin Richardson Vincent

Biblical Inspiration and Christ

Marvin Richardson Vincent

Biblical Inspiration and Christ

ISBN/EAN: 9783337182229

Printed in Europe, USA, Canada, Australia, Japan

Cover: Foto ©Lupo / pixelio.de

More available books at **www.hansebooks.com**

BIBLICAL INSPIRATION
AND CHRIST

BY

MARVIN R. VINCENT, D.D.

NEW YORK

ANSON D. F. RANDOLPH & COMPANY

(INCORPORATED)

182 FIFTH AVENUE

PRESS OF
EDWARD O. JENKINS' SON,
NEW YORK.

BIBLICAL INSPIRATION AND CHRIST.

THE church is not agreed as to the nature, extent and operations of Biblical inspiration. The discussions of the subject have produced a large crop of adjectives which are intended to serve as definitions. Out of the darkness occasionally comes a dogmatic thunder-clap announcing that this or that is indispensable to an orthodox conception of inspiration, but it is only thunder, and we are no better and no worse off than before.

HOW FAR IS DEFINITION POSSIBLE?

As to what inspiration is essentially, it is not likely that we can ever reach a definition, any more than we can reach a definition of life. The word "inspiration" tells us very little. It is merely *inbreathing*. It gives us no hint of the source or of the moral quality of that which is inbreathed. It may mean simply the imparting of the physical power of respiration. The meanings which are popularly assigned to it do not reside in the word, but attach to it through theological usage. The Greek word θεοπνευστία carries us a little farther. It tells us that the inbreathed force, whatever it be, is imparted by God, and thus indicates its essential moral quality. This is all. Neither word answers the question, what is the peculiar quality which we call inspiration, which differentiates the Bible from all other books and makes it authoritative as a rule of faith and practice?

For it is evident that if we confine ourselves to the words "inspiration," "ϑεοπνευστία," we still have no standard by which to distinguish the Bible from scores of other books. According to its primary meaning, inspiration is not confined to the Bible. It exists and works wherever God breathes life and power into men. A work of genius is inspired. A good life is inspired. A deed of heroism is an inspiration. St. John's gospel is inspired, but so are the Iliad, and Hamlet and the Divina Commedia. And yet it is entirely consistent with this to say that the peculiar quality of Biblical inspiration is higher than the inspiration of these works, and imparts to the Bible a character which belongs to none of them. What this peculiar element is, is the thing we want to know.

THE NATURE OF BIBLICAL INSPIRATION AN INDUCTION FROM THE ACTUAL PHENOMENA OF THE BIBLE.

In the discussion of this question we are thrown wholly and only upon the phenomena exhibited by the Bible itself. The Bible does not formally describe or define its own inspiration. It says nothing about its own quality as a book, for the simple reason that no Biblical writer is cognizant of the book as a whole. All that is possible for us is to collate the phenomena of the book, and to deduce from these our conception or definition of inspiration. Our final formula, moreover, whatever it be, must include all the phenomena. Especially, we cannot be allowed to start with any *a priori* hypothesis and attempt to fit the phenomena into this. In other words, we must not begin by saying, "inspiration, *in the nature of the case*, must be this or that. It must exclude this or include that." Such a process is not scientific but empirical, and can never lead to any substantial or reliable result. This is clearly shown by the history of physical science. So long as astronomers proceeded on the assumption that the earth was the stationary centre of the universe, or that the orbits of the planets must, in the nature of the case, be perfect circles, the way was barred to all correct scientific results. These assumptions had to be thrown out of the process of investigation before any real progress could be made. They ran against the facts at every point, and the attempt to adjust the facts to the assumptions resulted in absurdities and poetic fancies. It may indeed happen, now and then, that legitimate deductions from actual phenomena indicate the correctness of an *a priori* hypothesis : but such cases are not common, and when they occur, they only show that the hypothesis was a happy guess, and do not justify the process. To say that, in the nature of the case, Biblical inspiration must be this or that, is to beg the question at issue. The nature of the case is the very thing we want to know, and this is not fixed by the dogmatic assertions of individuals or of church councils. It can be determined, if determined at all, only by the facts. We must go as far as these carry us, and stop if they do not carry us as far as we may desire. Beyond that point we may speculate, but we must not dogmatize.

Let us consider some of the facts. We have in the Bible a book containing a certain revelation, largely historical, of the person and character of God, and of his purposes toward men—a revelation which is expressly designed to bring human nature into conformity with the divine character, to inform it with aspiration for this, and to furnish impulses and rules for its attainment.

A DISTINCTION BETWEEN REVELATION AND SCRIPTURE.

The Bible is a record, a medium, a vehicle of divine revelation ; but it is important that a distinction should be made between revelation and Scripture, though the two are intimately and necessarily associated. We must be especially careful not to identify them ; for from such identification it follows that a book is a necessity of a revelation, that the book must be co-extensive with the revelation, and that the revelation must be limited by the book. It follows that no character can attach to revelation which does not attach to the book: that the book is as complete, as purely divine, as unmixed with human error, passion, and infirmity as the revelation. It follows that the design of God in his revelation included the production of an immaculate book. Revelation, which is essentially divine, pure and inerrant, is inspired in the highest sense that can attach to that term. It is the very breath of God: the expression of the life of God. The identification of revelation and Scripture therefore implies that Scripture is inspired in the same sense, and that an inspired book means a faultless book.

A BOOK NOT A NECESSITY OF A REVELATION. REVELATION LARGER THAN ITS RECORD.

Now the phenomena of Scripture directly contradict these positions. In the first place they prove that a book is not a necessity of a revelation. On the testimony of the Bible itself, revelation is larger than its record. The Bible tells us of a revelation of God to men before there was any Bible, a revelation not conveyed by writing: a revelation given in divers manners—by direct communication of God with individuals, by visions, by symbols, by theophanies, by signs and wonders. We are told of Noah as the man who built the ark and survived the deluge ; but there is a whole unwritten history in the brief statement that Noah was perfect in his generations. We can only guess what is locked up in the words, "Enoch walked with God." There was a revelation of God through human deeds and human characters which is only hinted at in the Bible, and which, we may be sure, included much that is not even hinted at. Moreover, there has been a revelation of God, a revelation embracing new factors, since the canon of Scripture was closed, and which will continue to unfold until time shall end. Are we indeed to believe that the revelation of God in history is limited to the history of the Jewish nation and to the few side-glances at Gentile history? Is there no revelation in the history of nineteen centuries? Has there been no voice of God, no divine lesson in the rise and fall of empires, the vast social and moral revolutions, the career and wreck of dynasties since the last line of the New Testament was penned? Is the revelation of God through the church confined to the Jewish Church, and the Christian Church as portrayed in the book of Acts and the Epistles of Paul? As well say that a great man's biography is completed with the story of his infancy. A revelation grander in its proportions, wider in its sweep, richer in its fruits, has unfolded in the historic development of the Christian Church with its magnificent missionary and philanthropic enterprise, and its unequalled record of Christian heroism.

As to the revelation of God in science, the elaborate attempts to show that Scripture anticipates modern science are scarcely worth noticing. Scripture was not intended to teach science. It is indeed possible, as numerous examples have shown, that a quick observation of the phenomena of nature by untutored men in an unscientific age should detect and state results which modern science has traced to their causes and placed in their appropriate categories. Some such things we find in the Bible; but to assume from this that it was God's intention to incorporate into Scripture the germs of modern science is absurd. Where the Bible deals with physical science at all, it does so under contemporary limitations of scientific knowledge. The Psalmist is impressed with the glory of the starry heavens; so was Homer, only Homer did not know the Psalmist's God, and did not bring him into his beautiful picture in the Iliad. To the Psalmist the heavens declared the glory of God, and the firmament showed his handy-work; but the whole conception, though essentially and profoundly truthful, was poetic and not scientific in form. Where in the Bible can there be found any exhibition of the physical universe approaching in grandeur the revelations of the divine wisdom and glory furnished by modern astronomy?

THE MORAL REVELATION IN SCRIPTURE PROGRESSIVE.

The moral revelation contained in the Bible itself is progressive. In every age which it depicts there is a large element of reserve in the divine revelation. What was imparted to Christ's disciples in the upper chamber, was not and could not be given to the Israelites at the foot of Sinai. John could not have written his first Epistle on the morning when he recognized Jesus on the lake-shore What was tolerated and even approved by God in the days of the patriarchs was condemned by Christ. Abraham was the friend of God: God styled himself the God of Jacob; David was declared to be a man after God's own heart; yet the moral and spiritual level of Abraham and Jacob and David is lower than that of Paul and John. God advanced from a revelation through symbols to a revelation through the prophets; from a revelation through the prophets to a revelation through his Son. Each lower stage contained a premonition of the higher. Is it not intended, is it not one of the valuable fundamental truths of the Bible which we are asked to learn from the Bible and to use in shaping our conception of Revelation—that revelation is essentially progressive? Does not the Bible, while it holds up to us its own revelation, persistently point beyond itself and lead us to expect ever new and larger unfoldings of the life and truth which it presents?

THE BOOK NOT AS PURELY DIVINE AS THE REVELATION.

Or do the phenomena of Scripture testify that the book is as purely divine, as unmixed with human traits as the revelation of God? Assuredly not. Nothing can be plainer than that the morally perfect revelation commits itself to a morally imperfect human medium. The pure sunlight passes into the minster through windows which are stained, cracked, and obscured with dust and cobwebs. Light *is* imparted—the light of the sun. Men within the minster see, and the sunlight is no less sunlight because the windows transmit it imperfectly. If it were indispensable to vision that the eye should be as perfect as the light which it reflects, the world would be full of the blind, since scientists tell us that a perfect eye is rarely if ever found.

The facts of Scripture do not show that a book is a necessity of a revelation: they do not show that, if a book is used, the book must be as faultless as the revelation, or, like the revelation, simply and purely divine. They do not show that, in giving a revelation through Scripture, God contemplated the production of an immaculate book. If such was his purpose, we should be fully warranted in expecting to find indications of it in the book itself, and in the history of its transmission. Such a purpose would involve the most minute and careful supervision of the entire process of transmission, by word of mouth, by transcription, by printing, by translation. It is evident to the most superficial observation that no such supervision has been exercised: that the attitude of providence toward the preservation of textual accuracy, and verbal niceties, and correctness of translation has been that of comparative indifference. Errors of transcription and breaks in transmission have been suffered freely to intrude themselves. From the time of the composition of the New Testament books

BIBLICAL INSPIRATION AND CHRIST. 11

down to the fourth century, we are left without a
manuscript copy. For our evidence of the existence and
circulation and authoritativeness of those books during
that period we are thrown upon versions from unknown
originals, upon scattered notices and quotations in the
works of church fathers and Christian apologists, or
upon compilations or adaptations made by anti-Chris-
tian or partially Christian writers in the interest of phi-
losophic theories. At a very early date we find different texts in different sections of the church, and much
uncertainty as to what was to be received as authentic
and authoritative New Testament Scripture. In scores
of cases we are not, after the most laborious critical re-
search, absolutely certain as to the exact words of the
original text.

Or, to go farther back, the Old Testament Scripture
largely in use by Jews and Christians in the days of
Christ and of the Apostles, was the Septuagint or Greek
translation, which was by no means a faithful translation of the original Hebrew, often little better than a
paraphrase, sometimes almost unintelligible, and, in not
a few cases, intentionally garbled.

Thousands of Christians had no access to the Bible
except through the old Latin versions which were so
corrupt as to make necessary the revision of Jerome,
which is itself far from accurate. Thousands of English
readers have received their only knowledge of Scripture
from the versions of Tyndale, Wyclif, and the transla-
tors of 1611, not one of which was free from grave
errors. This is, of course, not to say that the Bible in
these forms has failed to convey the substantial truth
of God, or has not been a priceless treasure to his chil-

dren in all those centuries. It is only to say that such facts, and they might easily be multiplied, furnish no evidence of any minute, special superintendence with a view to preserving intact an originally immaculate book.

HUMAN ELEMENTS IN THE BIBLE.

Of the human elements which interpenetrate the Bible it would almost seem superfluous to speak. They emerge at every point. The revelation does not clothe itself in a unique language of its own. It takes and uses human language as it finds it. It draws for its imagery and illustration upon the familiar facts of nature and of human life. It casts the truth into the mould of the age to which it is originally addressed, suffers it to be colored and flavored by the local and temporary traits of that age, and to be expounded according to its literary methods. The human agents selected to transmit the revelation are not ideally holy and perfect men. They are stained with human infirmities and sometimes with human crimes. Certain of the Old Testament saints would be justly ostracized by Christian society. Certain of the Old Testament utterances blaze with a passion which is anything but a divine rapture, and hiss with imprecations which shock even an average moralist.

THE PRINCIPLE OF ACCOMMODATION IN SCRIPTURE.

Moreover, the revelation of God in Scripture does not hold an independent and transcendent course of its own. It does not move on wings above the heads of men, sweeping in a straight line to its end, but walks on foot by their side, climbing the heights, descending into the valleys, and following the winding paths along with them. It does not arbitrarily transcend natural laws and rates of development: rather it accommodates itself to these and suffers its movement to be retarded by them. It is supernatural, yet it follows a natural process. It is divine, yet it measures its pace by the rate of natural historic development. It is eternal, yet there is a fulness of time before which its great crises are not suffered to arrive. Its design is to make men holy and loving and noble, yet it does not achieve this result by a sudden and miraculous moral transformation. The rabble of Israelitish slaves is not lifted at a stroke out of the idolatries of Egypt and placed at the level of a Christian of the nineteenth century. The revelation of God in Christ is not given to Israel at Sinai. Naturally, it would have availed nothing. No miracle is wrought to make it immediately available. Centuries elapse before the Word is made flesh. The divine moral ideals finally enunciated by Christ, move slowly up towards realization through stages in which slavery and polygamy and retaliation and divorce are tolerated and encouraged ; in which the ferocity of barbarous warfare is suffered to take its course ; in which Israel is commanded to massacre the Canaanites, and Jael is praised as an agent of God, in a triumphal hymn, for a deed of hideous and treacherous cruelty.

ERRORS IN SCRIPTURE.

Again, the Scriptures bear the marks of human ignorance or inadvertence in certain of their statements. The Bible is not literally and verbally inerrant. It contains errors of detail, discrepancies of number and date and fact. Grant that these errors are trifling and

do not affect the substantial value and truthfulness of
the record as a whole: on the assumption that a divine
revelation implies an immaculate record as its necessary
complement, they present a very serious difficulty.
They cannot be gotten over or explained away by any
means at our command : and if the truthfulness and
value of the revelation is dependent upon such a fact
as this, the revelation must abandon its high claim. To
meet such an issue by the assertion that, whatever the
present condition of the record, the original autographs
were absolutely without flaw, is a desperate resource
which requires no discussion. To base a positive dogma
upon a statement which there are no means of verify-
ing, upon the character of documents which have no
existence, is to fly in the face not only of sound logic,
but of common sense. It is high time that such arguments (by courtesy so called) should be abandoned by
men who profess to be scholars and thinkers. God can
make something out of nothing ; but the combined theologians, theological schools, and ecclesiastical councils
of all time cannot make a valid argument for the verbal
inerrancy of Scripture out of documents which it is impossible for any one to consult. For all such it remains
true that "*ex nihilo nihil fit.*"

It is thus apparent that a divine revelation must not
be identified with its record, however intimately and
necessarily associated with it : that a revelation which
is wholly and essentially divine may ally itself for purposes of transmission or for other purposes with a medium which is not wholly divine. If the medium
must be as divine and faultless as the revelation,
which is the expression of God's own thought and will,

then the conception of Biblical inspiration must include immaculateness, inerrancy, and accordingly the Bible, tested by its own phenomena, is not inspired, and is not a proper vehicle of a divine revelation. If divine revelation includes the intent to make an inerrant book, the intent of divine revelation has not been carried out. If all of divine revelation is included in the Bible, the larger portion of human history contains no revelation of God. On the contrary, there is a large margin on either side of the book which teems with revelation. That the book has definite and important relations to this margin, that it may furnish the key to the interpretation of the history which precedes and follows the Bible, that it may teach us to discern God in history everywhere,—may be freely granted: but the facts already cited create enormous difficulties for one who begins by assuming that the Bible is the only revelation of God, and that the nature of its inspiration includes and demands an immaculate record.

If then inspiration does not consist in or require inerrancy, perfect consistency of detail, systematic statement and development of doctrine, transmission through men of perfect character, utterances wholly divine in spirit and word—where shall we seek for the spiritual force which makes the Bible the book of books, the authoritative rule of faith and practice? Where is lodged the transcendent quality of the Bible which warrants us in calling it inspired?

PERSONALITY THE CENTRAL FACTOR OF INSPIRATION.

We are at least safe in saying that inspiration is the Spirit of God informing the life, the work, and the

word of men. It is not confined to documents. A holy
deed is as truly inspired as a holy gospel or epistle.
One element is indispensable. Inspiration must involve personality both in the inspirer and the inspired.
Nothing impersonal can inspire or be inspired. A
document is not inspired in its letters and words, but in
the imparted personality of him who writes it. This
element must be central to any truthful conception of
inspiration, and to this we shall devote the remainder
of the discussion.

THE PERSONAL GOD IN THE OLD TESTAMENT.

It goes without saying that the element of divine
personality—the direct, sharply-defined, emphasized
energy of the personal God—pervades Scripture.
Scripture treats history, not as a natural evolution of
physical and psychological laws, but as the development of a divine purpose. It is the story of the contact of the personal God with humanity. Its dominant
idea is God's effort to make man godlike. In secular
history religion is incidental. In Biblical history it is
central. Scripture history illustrates God's dealing
with man in selection, in guidance, in pardon and pun-
ishment, in spiritual education, in national triumph,
disaster, and humiliation, in redemption and restora-
tion. The Bible is full of God's yearning and striving
to breathe his own Spirit into the thought, the feeling,
the activity, the literary product, the social and domes-
tic life, the national ideals, and the jurisprudence of the
race. It is not the working of an abstract " power not
ourselves which makes for righteousness " that this history portrays. A moral power without personality is,

in any case, a philosophical absurdity; and the vast movement of Hebrew history is neither propelled nor controlled by an abstraction. The Hebrew Scriptures —not only in their substance, but in their language with its bold anthropomorphisms, in their dramatic vividness, in their startling and sublime theophanies,— are alive with the presence and activity of the personal Jehovah. Where modern thought would put second causes, the Old Testament puts the First Cause. Where modern representations, even with a distinct conscious- ness of a higher, supernatural agency, would put the natural agent, or the farmer, the general, the states- man into the foreground,—in the Bible representation God clothes his hands with lightning and flings the flash across the sky; God empties his urns on the hill- tops, and sends the streams down into the valleys; God covers the pastures with flocks and makes the corn- lands stand thick with waving ears. God in person conducts the campaigns of Barak and of Gideon, and draws the fatal cordon round Jericho. Abraham's mi- gration is not the mere natural impulse of a restless nomad: God calls him into the strange country. God arranges the nuptials of Isaac, peoples Jacob's sleep at Bethel with visions, and grapples with him at Jabbok.

So it is throughout. No sense of the transcendent majesty of God runs into a sense of his remoteness. Every Hebrew is trained to believe in his personal presence in camp and in city, and to expect his direct interference in the most ordinary details. God burns in glory upon the ark, and overshadows the tabernacle with his cloud; yet he directs the manufacture of curtains and fringes, of rings, knops, and flowers. He

drives back the Red Sea, yet he prescribes all the
minute sanitary details of the Levitical code. Nay,
the sense of his divine majesty is appealed to in order
to heighten the sense of his minute and special care;
as in the Pilgrim Psalm, where the Maker of heaven
and earth comes down from the mountains into the
camp, the keeper of all Israel, yet mounting guard
over a single sleeper's tent.

HUMAN PERSONALITY IN SCRIPTURE.

A corresponding emphasis upon human personality
appears throughout Scripture. The main thrust of the
divine energy is upon man, upon human character.
Men constitute the fibre of the Bible, men in their different relations to the divine purpose and working.
Mere precept is comparatively impotent apart from
personality. Detach their exhortations, command-
ments, denunciations from the personalities of Moses,
David, Samuel, and Elijah; take them out of their
historical setting and throw them into categories—and
the main force of their appeal is gone. Accordingly,
through the entire Bible there runs a line of represent-
ative men, chosen organs of the inspiration of the
Almighty, kindled and guided by his Spirit. "The
life is the light of men." The chief appeal of the
Bible is through men. The power and the inspiration
of the Bible are not in naked precept, though the precept be divine, but in the incarnation of precept in
heroic and holy lives: not in the poetic beauties of
Hebrew song as divinely dictated words, but in its un-
folding of the longing, the ecstasy, the penitence, the
humiliation, the love, and the hope of human souls,

bared to the touch of God, and responding to the revelations of his character and will; not in the minute
correspondence of events with prophetic details, but in
the penetrating moral insight of divinely-moved men
into the moral tendencies of their age, and their persist-
ent pointing to the divine principles of conduct and
life.

THE MOVEMENT OF THE DIVINE ENERGY IN SCRIPTURE AFFECTED AND MODIFIED BY ITS HUMAN MEDIA.

An important fact at this point, already fore-
shadowed, is that the movement of this divine, personal energy in Scripture, is affected and modified
by the human media through which it operates. The
divine force recognizes, accepts, and to a very consider-
able extent, accommodates itself to these limitations.
Inspiration is content to work through such men as it
finds, while it none the less works to educate and to
sanctify the men. It does not wait for perfect men.
It glows in Abraham and Jacob and Moses with a
power distinctly recognized by the New Testament
writer who catalogues them as examples for the Christian Church. None the less it is apparent, and Scripture is at no pains to conceal or to palliate the fact,
that the inspiration goes hand in hand with moral infirmity. We have the twenty-third Psalm, and we
have David the seducer and murderer. We have
Elijah, magnificent on Carmel, and pitiable under the
juniper tree. We have Jacob, a vulgar trickster at
Beersheba and Padan Aram, and a prince of God at
Jabbok. We have Abraham's faith on Moriah and
Abraham's lie in Egypt. We have God's own testi-

mony to the uprightness of Job, and Job's frenzied challenge of Almighty justice. Inspiration consents to ally itself with that which is morally inferior to its own divine quality, with a human element which it lifts and guides and uses, but which it refuses to suppress or to crush.

Accordingly the quality of the men imparts itself to their utterances. If we view the writings apart from the men, and apart from their historical conditions, we find it difficult to reconcile them with any of the traditional theories of Biblical inspiration. They reflect the spiritual and moral limitations and imperfections of their authors. The imprecatory Psalms with their dreadful words of vengeance and their withering curses are in the canon along with the Sermon on the Mount. No forcing process, however vigorous or ingenious, can wrench the Psalms into harmony with the Sermon. The only possible solution of the inconsistency lies in the clear recognition of the historic consciousness in Scripture, in the recognition that revelation is progressive ; in the perception of the sharp distinction between the historic and the preceptive ; between what is fixed and what is in movement toward fixedness ; between eternal, immutable, divine canons, and the education of wayward human wills ; between wayside landmarks in the history of moral and spiritual progress, and ultimate standards of character ; above all, in the perception of the large element of human personality in Scripture, working alongside of the divine, and at once employed, tolerated, and educated in its contact with the divine.

If, in other words, we read the Bible as a history of

the growth of divine principles and character in men, of
the progressive operation of divine grace upon men, as a
record of the successive stages by which humanity has
been pushed Godward—if we consent to study inspiration in persons rather than in documents, or in documents
chiefly as informed with personality, then it will not
be hard to find in Scripture a legitimate place and
function for utterances which exhibit the grade and
quality of the moral sentiment generated and tolerated
in the " times of ignorance" which " God overlooked."
Then the Christian reader, putting himself for the
time at the historic level of the men who could pray
with such vengeful thoughts and scorching words, will
discern in those words that which God has caused to be
recorded for his instruction and warning—a tide-mark
in the rise of spiritual culture, and a finger-post pointing away from itself toward a purer moral ideal.

I have already spoken of that other feature of the
limitations incident to transmission of divine revelation
through human media, namely, that inspiration works
through the ordinary individual methods and agencies
of men. This is not to say that it never transcends
them, but that the Bible as a whole comes to us stamped
with the intellectual and moral characteristics of the
writers of its different books, and clothed in the forms
peculiar to the different ages in which they were written. On this it is unnecessary to dwell.

All such facts accentuate the personal element of inspiration—the divine Spirit's residence and operation in
men. They show that the Spirit refuses to relinquish
this medium because of limitations, intellectual or
moral. The transcendent quality of Scripture does not

reside in verbal inerrancy, in consistency of detail, or in
quality of phraseology and style as Coleridge remarks.
There may be dictation without inspiration, and inspiration without dictation. Balaam's ass was the passive
organ of divine dictation, but no one would think of
calling the animal inspired. Inspiration does not turn
on the agreement or disagreement between Samuel and
Kings as to the number of horses which David took
from Hadadezer, or as to whether David destroyed seven
hundred or seven thousand chariots of the Syrians. It
matters little whether Luke may or may not have made
a slip as to Cyrenius, or that Matthew has put Jeremiah
for Zechariah, or that Stephen's speech does not tally
accurately with the narrative in Genesis. It matters
nothing that Peter's Greek will not stand the tests of
the Attic grammarians, or that Paul's Epistles are full
of anacolutha and unclosed parentheses. Over and past
all such trifles we are carried by the sense of God in
the men; as we see how they are dominated and swept
onward by zeal for God, though their zeal sometimes
finds expression in forms from which the Christian
sense revolts: as we see how clearly they discern the
facts and principles of the unseen world as the only
eternal verities; how they are possessed and burdened
with its divine themes and goaded by its divine impulses until human words and symbols are strained to
the breaking-point.

" PROPHECY THE CENTRAL PHENOMENON OF SCRIPTURE."

This is the characteristic of prophecy: " *Men* spake
from God, being borne along by the Holy Spirit."
" Prophecy," as Professor Sanday remarks, " is the central phenomenon of Scripture." Prophecy is, primarily,

instruction; not merely and not principally prediction. It is forth-telling rather than fore-telling. "The most outstanding feature of prophecy," to quote the words of Professor Bruce, "to which all others must be subordinated, and by which all others are best understood, is its ethical character. The prophets were not principally foretellers or prognosticators of future events, and whatever predictions occur in their writings, and whatever use can be made of these for evidential purposes, the *raison d'être* of this remarkable class of religious teachers was not to supply materials for the apologist. The prophets were, before all things, preachers of righteousness and mercy to Israel, specially to their contemporaries in Israel. . . . . In all they say and do in fulfilment of their vocation, their obvious aim is to make a moral impression on the men among whom they live. . . . . In uttering their predictions they have not in view men living in ages after, using these as arguments for the truth of revelation, but people nearer themselves, sinners and saints living in the same land, as their neighbors and fellow-countrymen. They are emphatically preachers to their own time, and they express themselves in the language best fitted to impress their contemporaries, depicting the future in colors adapted to their circumstances, so that from their style you can form a guess as to their age. . . . . Evermore the future is described so as to suit the present need, and harmonize with the surroundings and the hopes and fears of the men to whom the prophetic message is primarily addressed, and on whom it is meant to act as a source of inspiration." ("The Chief End of Revelation," p. 197.)

Whether in the form of psalmody, wisdom, ritual, or

oracle, the instruction is prophecy. Moses is a prophet
no less than Isaiah ; the unknown author of Ecclesiastes
as well as Ezekiel. The prophets are organs of the divine Spirit. They are styled "Servants of God" and
"men of the Spirit." Their close fellowship with God
is asserted, and their word is his word :

> " Surely Adonai Jehovah doeth nothing
> Unless he hath revealed his secret plan
> To his servants the prophets." *

They do not assume this office voluntarily, but under
strong divine constraint, and sometimes reluctantly
(Exod. iv. 1–12). They bring to bear upon the social
and political conscience of their own age the great,
divinely-revealed ideals of righteousness, truth, and
mercy ; and by these ideals they measure and forecast
national prosperity and national decadence. The pre-
dictive element, which is the smallest element in their
utterances, is, in great part, the result of a clear discern-
ment of divine principles and of their inevitable bear-
ings. In the light of these principles they detect the
trend and the issue of contemporary tendencies ; but
there are points where their vision of the future seems
to transcend natural limits. Such knowledge and forecast and sharpened insight as might characterize a Mac-
chiavelli or a Bismarck, operate side by side with higher
and more mysterious phenomena of the divine afflatus.

We who know the prophets only through their writings, are in danger of overlooking the power of their
personality, and of forgetting how largely the force of
their appeal to their age lay in that. Rebuke and warn-

---

* Amos iii. 7, 8. See Professor Briggs' "Messianic Prophecy,"
p. 16.

ing, prediction and denunciation wrought their effects through the living voice, the familiar form, the play of the well-known features, the symbolic acts. They were felt as Moses dashed down the tables of the law; as Elijah called down fire upon Carmel; as Jeremiah broke the bottle in the valley of Hinnom.

THE MESSIANIC ELEMENT IN PROPHECY.

Again, the great gulf-stream of prophecy is the Messianic current; the growing ideal of the Messiah-King, his work and his kingdom. All the principles and features of the divine administration expounded by the prophets are in process of development towards his personal reign. All the mandates of the divine will, all the yearnings of the divine heart are expanding into the full flower of Messianic fulfilment. This is the ideal which informs the love and hope and faith and desire of the Old Testament saints, the ideal conceived under the forms and conditions of their own age, and which gives its specific and essential character to the redemption which they expound, and the full glory of which they await.

The phenomena of inspiration, as it thus reveals itself through human media, all fall, therefore, into a common movement towards a consummate expression which shall exhibit inspiration as no less the divine impress on human personality, but at its full power, unfettered by the intellectual crudity and moral infirmity with which it has all along struggled. The Spirit of God tolerates and uses imperfect media, but always with a forward look towards a higher expression in the perfect manhood of Jesus Christ. The later phase of Biblical inspiration is thus true to the direction of

its whole earlier drift. The inspired personality of
Jesus, "full of the Holy Ghost," though in itself
unique, is the consummate development of a movement
which has been from the beginning associated with
human personality. The whole stream of Old Testament revelation has been sweeping onward from God
in man to the God-man. The entire history of " men
moved by the Holy Ghost," culminates in "the Word
made flesh."

THE TESTIMONY OF JESUS IS THE SPIRIT OF PROPHECY.

When we have reached this point, we hold the key
to the inspiration of Scripture. As we have seen that
prophecy is the central phenomenon of Scripture, we
now see that Jesus is the central phenomenon of
prophecy: that "the testimony of Jesus is the spirit
of prophecy." As prophecy works all along through
personality, so Jesus incarnates the spirit and the substance of prophecy in a perfect personality. Into himself he gathers up all that is vital and eternal in
prophecy, whether in psalm, ritual, or wisdom. Moses,
the prophet of the law, is first fully interpreted by
Christ the fulfiller of the law. " Beginning from
Moses and all the prophets," he interprets "in all the
Scriptures the things concerning himself." " The
Scriptures," he declares, " testify of me." He repre-
sents at once the divine energy and the consummate result of inspiration. He is a man speaking from God
and moved by the Holy Spirit. All that is essentially
divine in Old Testament personality appears in him in
full manifestation, in new, wider, and more varied relations, and in perfect symmetry. The divine impulses

which come upon Old Testament prophets in occasional,
transient gusts, breathe upon him with a steady and
uniform intensity.

JESUS AND THE NEW TESTAMENT.

It becomes the more evident, as we study the New
Testament, that the personality of Christ is so woven
into its fibre that it cannot be detached without the ut-
ter ruin of the New Testament regarded as a document. The words of Jesus are indeed "spirit and
life," but they are so as he speaks them. They are inspired as his words. The New Testament is unique
in that its moral and spiritual value as a group of writings is absolutely dependent upon this divine personality. It might help us to a better understanding of
Plato if we could know Plato as we know Christ. It
does help us that we know something of Socrates.
But that makes little difference after all. Whatever
Plato's thought can do for us, it does without Plato
himself. It would do as much under any other name
or under no name. But Christ's words are comparatively impotent without him. Whatever may or may
not be essential to the exhibition of abstract truth or
of physical science, incarnation is a necessity of a
divine revelation of moral and spiritual truth. The
ideas of such a revelation refuse to be divorced from
personality. Sin, pardon, faith, love, hope, holiness,
will, conscience,—all are personal; and the essence of
Christianity is the entrance of a new spiritual consciousness, a new will, a new affection, a new personality in short, into human nature.

JESUS INTERPRETS THE OLD TESTAMENT.

Having reached this point, we find that the light is
thrown back from it upon the previous revelation.
Recurring to the imperfect media which divine inspiration selected as its own vehicles, and to the large
amount of human crudity, ignorance, and moral infirmity
which attach to these, we find at once an apology for
the fact (if one be needed), a corrective, and an abso-
lute standard by which to test the utterances of man or
document. Christ himself states the apology for certain features of the legal revelation on the ground of
rudimentary moral conditions which God suffered to
work themselves out, and did not choose to abolish by
miracle. With equal distinctness, however, he asserts
that such conditions were not according to the divine
archetype. "Moses, for the hardness of your hearts,
suffered you to put away your wives; but from the beginning it hath not been so." *

And Christ asserts himself as the corrector of such
features of the legal dispensation. "Ye have heard
that it was said by them of old time . . . . but I say
unto you." That is final. The other is only temporary and provisional. "An eye for an eye and a tooth
for a tooth" has no place in the Sermon on the Mount.
The spirit of Elijah is rebuked in John and James.
The vengeful words of the imprecatory Psalms are out
of tune with "Bless them that curse you," and "Forgive us our debts as we forgive our debtors."

* Matt. xix. 8.

THE CLUE TO THE CONTINUITY OF THE REVELATION
AND TO THE INSPIRATION OF SCRIPTURE IS IN
CHRIST'S PERSON.

As we take our stand beside Christ and look backward, we now for the first time apprehend the continuity of the revelation and the inspiration of Scripture, and grasp the clue to it in his person. God in Christ is not a fact for the first time at Bethlehem. "God *was* in Christ, reconciling the world unto himself." As Augustine puts it, " Christianity is as old as the world." The Word " was in the beginning "—the Word embodying the two prime factors of inspiration, life and light, and "the life was the light of men." Therefore Christ " corresponds to the whole tenor of the Scriptures of the past. The Hebrews who wistfully look back to their temple, law, and ritual, are not taught a stern forgetfulness of what had been, nor led vaguely to spiritualize its meaning, but are led to realize, in each part of the ancient system, a line which leads up to Christ." *

The Old Testament stream thus debouches into the New, leaving its banks strewn with broken types, obsolete ordinances, empty shells of symbol, moral accommodations, but carrying with it the great personal factor of its inspiration,—God in man, living, speaking, writing. Prophecy is the dominant factor of the New Testament as of the Old. Still, only in a more pronounced and apprehensible sense, " the testimony of Jesus is the spirit of prophecy." Prophecy is a charisma of the apostolic church, but its testimony

* E. S. Talbot in " Lux Mundi."

must be to Christ, or it is spurious. The Spirit continues to move men, but the Spirit that refuses to confess that Christ is come in the flesh is not of God. New Testament prophecy is not only testimony to Christ, it is the testimony of Christ. The prophetic gift is identified with Christ as its dispenser and regulative standard. John declares that Jesus imparts the Spirit in his fulness.* Faith in Christ as the sphere and subjective condition of the power and function of believers, defines the proportion in which the prophetic endowment is shared (Rom. xii. 3, 6). Peter ascribes the outpouring of the Spirit at Pentecost directly to Christ (Acts ii. 32, 33); and Paul affirms that to apostles, prophets, evangelists, pastors and teachers grace is dispensed according to the measure of the gift of Christ (Eph. iv. 7–11). That which makes prophecy the living reflection of the mind of God, is the testimony of Jesus. That through which the Spirit of God acts in prophecy to reprove, edify, comfort, and convict, is the testimony of Jesus. That which makes the fulfilment of prophecy other and more than a mere mechanical correspondence of event with prediction, and which exhibits event and prediction as alike factors of a moral and spiritual development in human history, is the testimony of Jesus. That which makes prophecy spirit instead of letter, which lifts its inspiration above the literal accuracy and peculiar structure of a document, which makes itself felt in what is anonymous or pseudonymous no less than in what is authentic, which concentrates attention upon the light

* John iii. 34. The correct reading omits ὁ θεός as the subject of δίδωσιν, so that the subject is " Christ " ὃν ἀπέστειλεν ὁ θεός.

rather than upon the lantern, and which, ignoring verbal discrepancy and mistaken or imperfect science, blazes through all with divine radiance, searching the conscience and analyzing the thoughts and intents of the heart—is the testimony of Jesus.

THE PERSONALITY OF JESUS AT ITS HIGHEST POWER UNDER THE DISPENSATION OF THE SPIRIT.

This fact does not receive its final emphasis in the earthly personality of Jesus. That emphasis comes with his withdrawal from earthly conditions. Thus only can personality finally and fully enter into Biblical inspiration at its highest power. The gospel narrative makes it evident that the immediate disciples of Jesus need a radical moral transformation and a larger spiritual outlook, before his personality can become in them an inspiration with a power of universal appeal. The Christian disciple who can say, " For me to live is Christ," is still in the future.

The ministry of the Holy Spirit was announced by Jesus as something far larger, richer, mightier and more fruitful than his ministry in the flesh, but none the less as peculiarly his own ministry. It inaugurated a new and distinct development in the character and work of the apostles, but the development was upon the same line, in that it was still a revelation and communication of his personal power. He plainly declared that the sum and substance of the Spirit's testimony should be himself; and that, in the coming and working of the Spirit he should come and work. The personality of Jesus, though withdrawn from sight and touch, now, for the first time, displays its un-

trammeled energy in the speech and writings of his
disciples. He is not only the theme, but the inspiring
force of their preaching. He preaches through them,
writes in their letters, and lives and works in their con-
secrated life and deeds. He pervades Peter's pente-
costal sermon and Peter's transformed manhood. He
is the momentum of Paul's splendid missionary career.
He speaks in the rhythmical swell of the Ephesian
letter, the involved parentheses of Romans, and the
tumultuous diction of Second Corinthians. His resur-
rection is not only a memory and a hope, but also a
continuous power in the Apostle to the Gentiles.
Paul's suffering is fellowship with Christ: his knowledge is summed up in Christ: his life is Christ. In
brief, the whole magnificent impulse and victorious
energy of the apostolic church is personal,—men
speaking and working and enduring as moved by the
Holy Ghost, and the testimony of Jesus the spirit of
their prophecy. Their manual is the Old Testament,
chiefly as it testifies of Christ. How little attention
they bestowed upon the question of its structure and
its verbal accuracy is apparent in their free use of the
Septuagint with all its blunders of translation and in-
tentional modifications of the Hebrew text, and in their
citations in forms which verbally correspond to neither
Hebrew nor Septuagint. Without any apparent consciousness of a scholastic theory of inspiration, they
recognize the fact and the essential quality of inspiration. By no one is this more clearly expressed than by
Peter, the last man in the world to concern himself
with any scientific conception or definition of *theo-
pneustia*. The Old Testament prophets, he says, caught

glimpses of a fulness of messianic salvation in the future.
The revealing agent was Christ himself; and in their
careful study of these hints and foregleams—of "what
time or what manner of time the spirit of Christ which
was in them did point unto"—they came to see that
their own ministry was to expand into a later and
larger ministry, in which other prophets would preach
that same Christ under the power of the same spirit of
Christ which inspired them (1 Pet. i. 10–12). That remarkable passage is simply the expansion of the words,
"the testimony of Jesus is the spirit of prophecy."

THE SPIRIT OF JESUS IN SCRIPTURE THE STARTING POINT
OF A TRUTHFUL CONCEPTION OF INSPIRATION.

This must be the starting-point of any conception of
Biblical inspiration that shall at once interpret its
nature and include all its phenomena: the spirit of
Jesus, speaking in the Scriptures of both dispensations,
and imparting to them their searching spiritual analysis, their power over the conscience, their profound insight into the truths of the kingdom of God, their
divine quality of instruction, comfort, and moral stimu-
lus: Jesus, in these expressions of his personal, divine
energy, foreshadowing in earlier prophecy his later,
grander, sweeter revelation—Jesus is the spirit, the
essential potency, the inspiration of Scripture. If we
begin with the scholastic descriptions and definitions of
inspiration, we get nowhere. If we begin with Jesus,
we do not need these. Take the much discussed words
in the third chapter of second Timothy, and how much
do they tell us about inspiration from the scholastic
point of view? How they rather strike at once into

the very marrow of the thing. "Every Scripture that is filled with the breath of God is profitable for teach-ing, for confutation, for setting to rights, for discipline in righteousness, for making a complete man, thor-oughly furnished unto every good work." Each of these elements of profitableness is perfectly embodied and wholly efficient only as Scripture works through Christ. In other words, Scripture exerts its highest power to teach, reprove, correct, discipline, and perfect, only through the personal Christ.

IS THIS CONCEPTION INDEFINITE?

It may be said that this conception is indefinite. It is so only in contrast with the artificial and superficial precision of scholastic definitions. If to be definite is to be literal, mechanical, reducible to the limits of such phrases as "plenary," "verbal," "inerrant," "dy-namic," and the like,—then the conception is indefinite, and the thing itself is indefinite, even as are the most po-tent forces of the kingdom of God; even as God himself. The operations of the Spirit of God, how-ever cognizable, refuse to confine themselves within formulas. Man knoweth not the way of the Spirit. Life cannot be formulated. The movement in history and in Scripture of such a personality as Christ's can-not be expressed by $x+y+z$. If Biblical inspiration can be wholly run into the formulas of the schools, if it can be shut up within the lines of an *a priori* con-ception of verbal or scientific accuracy, it is too small to work on the same plane with its gigantic sister-forces. As well expect a cyclone to pick its way between the beds of a kitchen-garden, as that this majestic, personal, divine energy, moving with its colossal stride through Scripture, should mince its pace over Matthew's mistake of Jeremiah for Zechariah, or the discrepancy between Stephen and Genesis, or the differences of the four Evangelists in recording the inscription over the cross. It is with Scripture as with nature. No one can define or formulate the divine life-force which animates its infinite varieties, or the impression which these combined varieties produce. Who can say in what consists the impression of beauty and power and restfulness produced by the forest on a bright morning in summer, as one walks along a road with the woods on either side, and spreading their boughs above his head like the groined arches of a cathedral? Certain elements of beauty are obvious—light, shadow, form, color, sound, perfume—but no possible combination of these alone will reproduce the impression of the forest. There are other elements beside these which appeal to a subtler sense, and the elements are not aggregated, but blended and fused in a way which defies analysis. All the elements are not beautiful according to our ideas of beauty : all the combinations are not symmetrical according to our canons of symmetry. Some things are wanting which we would have added if we had been making a forest : some things are there which we would have left out. The forest is not geometrically laid out. It is not made up of straight lines and perfect curves and correct angles. There are knots and gnarls, branches crossed and distorted and interlaced, tangled underbrush, rotting trunks, broken limbs, fungi and parasites. These, no less than the light and the perfume and the color, enter into the general effect.

So, after the component factors of Scripture have been reduced to their last analysis, something remains which defies analysis, and which is greater and more impressive than all the factors combined. Its beauty and power cannot be reduced to theological categories or measured by grammatical, philological, historical, or logical standards. It is not a photograph of our ideal men or of our ideal society. It contains much which, if we had been making a Bible, we would have omitted. It sets at defiance critical canons which we would never have dared to violate. It is full of dark passages, gnarled and twisted humanities, broken and tangled histories, crooked logic, fragments which cannot be pieced together according to any artificial harmony, relics of extinct life, traces of the growth and transformations of centuries: but though there are thickets through which we cannot cut a way, bends which we cannot straighten, fragments which we cannot complete,— through the midst of all lies a road on which the mingled light and perfume and song—the whole sweet, exalting, restful power of the Word—come out to him who walks it in simple faith, THE WAY, Jesus Christ.

FALSE LIMITATIONS.

There are those whose ideal of Scripture is like the old French ideal of landscape gardening; avenues of stiff poplars, and trees and hedges trimmed into figures of men and beasts. They would clip with their dogmatic shears the great cedars of Lebanon which the Lord hath planted, and trim the luxuriant foliage into theological hobgoblins, and train the clustering vines over doctrinal trellises, and then affirm that the clip-

ping and the hogoblins and the stiff trellises represent
the Bible. Such is the Bible of the schools—a thing
which is without inspiration, and which mocks and car-
icatures God and nature and truth ; an enclosure where
scholastic entomologists and botanists are ever making
up their collections of dead flies and their herbaria of
dead leaves ; where literalism has struck at life, and
petty verbal theories have tainted the fresh, bracing
breath of the Spirit with the poison of the parching
Sarsar wind.

Biblical inspiration, in its large and true sense, rejects
these limitations. They neutralize any force which the
appeal of the Bible might otherwise carry for non-Chris-
tian scholars and thinkers. Whenever this literal and
verbal mania has had its full swing, it has issued in the
grossest absurdities and the most fantastic freaks of exe-
gesis ; in the vagaries of allegory, the monstrosities of
the Talmud, the fancies of Philo, the extravagances of
Origen and Clement, the assertion of the divine inspiration of the Hebrew vowel-points and accents, and the
Purist dogma that to speak of barbarisms and solecisms
in New Testament Greek is blasphemy against the Holy
Ghost.

Such puerilities are not confined to the past. The
Helvetic consensus contains nothing worse than can be
found in the speech of the Rev. Dr. Birch during
the trial of Dr. Briggs by the Presbytery of New York.
He says: "In the Sermon on the Mount, Jesus Christ
not only denies the statements of the Inaugural, that
there is nothing divine in the *letters*, words, and clauses
of the Bible, but *he goes further than that*. Listen to
him : 'Think not that I am come to destroy the law or

the prophets. I am not come to destroy, but to fulfil. For verily I say unto you, Till heaven and earth pass, one jot or one tittle shall in no wise pass from the law until all be fulfilled.'" After quoting Bishop Ellicott's explanation of the words "jot" and "tittle," he proceeds : "It was possible, by the neglect or misuse of the jot or tittle, to turn divine truth into nonsense or blasphemy. Hence, if the law is of a piece with the whole Bible, there can be nothing superfluous or insignificant in that Bible. *The jot and tittle are as divine as the concepts!* The Inaugural's line of distinction between the essentials and the circumstantials is pronounced by the Bible to be an error. You cannot separate, as to divine inspiration, between the religion, faith, and morals of the Bible, and its other characteristics, for example, language, geography, history. If we cannot trust the *ipsissima verba* of the divine writings when we want to learn the divine will, 'what is there,' asks another, 'that we can trust?' And he goes on to say : 'One jot, one *yod*, a little thing, that is not a letter in itself so much as the adjunct and helper of another —a *yot*, a silent thing. The wife of Abraham was turned from Sarai to Sarah, and it was the *yod* that did it : it was that little, silent, insignificant adjunct that turned her into Princess. *God is careful of his yod or yot or jot. He does not dot his i for nothing, nor cross his t merely for decoration.*'" *

Comment is needless. On one point Dr. Birch is absolutely and fatally right. No one has ever more conclusively demonstrated that "it is possible, by the

* The quotation is from the authorized printed report of the speech. Most of the italics are mine.

misuse of the jot or tittle, to turn divine truth into nonsense."

If, on the other hand, Biblical inspiration be referred for its definition and verification to its personal factor, to the power communicated by men speaking under the impulse of the Holy Ghost, and conveying therefore the testimony of Jesus, the standard of reference is definite and apprehensible. It is not rendered less definite by the recognition in Scripture of the human element with all that attaches to it. If the divine in Scripture cannot transcend human limitation and imperfection, even where it suffers them to appear and speak, it proclaims itself less than divine. If the flavor and quickening power of the draught are inseparable from the perfection of the goblet; if a proved error in Scripture contradicts the Scripture claims and therefore its inspiration in making those claims, we must give up inspiration. The dogma of inerrancy is in the teeth of facts on the very face of the Bible, and apparent to any competent student of its originals.

THE QUESTION OF INSPIRATION NOT ESOTERIC.

Moreover, it may well be asked what is the nature of the appeal which a sound theory of inspiration may make to the average mind. This is no light matter, to be summarily dismissed with the assertion that it is of little consequence that the average mind should have a definite conception of the nature of inspiration, so long as it accepts Scripture as the word of God and the rule of faith and practice. That this is, largely, the attitude of the average mind may be granted, as it may be granted that such a mind may draw rules of life and spiritual help and comfort from the Bible without having a theory of its inspiration or giving any thought to that matter. Men lived long before the science of biology. But unless the subject is essentially unintelligible, in which case it has no claim upon any mind, it may be confidently affirmed that the hold of Scripture upon the average mind will be strengthened by some intelligent notion of the meaning and character of its inspiration.

It has been too generally assumed that the question of inspiration is esoteric—a question for scholars and theologians only ; and that assumption has gained ground from the fact that the appeal of the scholastic theories is, and must be, mainly to unintelligent belief. If inspiration is essentially a question of philology, if it is bound up with verbal inerrancy and accurate correspondence of detail, such matters can be settled by scholars only. Practically, inspiration means, to the great mass of uneducated Christians, verbal dictation, mechanical transcription, and supernatural combination. It is a thing of the letter and not of the spirit, something which is accepted on authority, which carries with it no spiritual quickening, but remains a mere dogmatic explanation of the process of manufacture, quite outside the sphere of spiritual activity. " Verbal inspiration," to quote the words of Henry Wood,* has been held as a protective doctrine, but its power to promote spiritual and moral energy is wanting. It has been relied upon more as a security and authority for doctrinal belief, than as a force to quicken life. Every sect has used it as an armor to defend its partic-

* "God's Image in Man."

ular tenets, more than as an energizing motive and
tonic. The prevailing conception of the book has been
rigid in form but deficient in vitality. It has been
held sacred as a source of correct theology, but its
power to infuse God-consciousness is largely unrecog-
nized. Its spiritual energy is the highest and only test
of its divine truthfulness, while verbal inerrancy is a
technicality, and invites attention to the letter that
killeth rather than to the spirit which giveth life. Ancient history, law, and prophecy, and also the teaching
of Christ and his apostles, must be translated into
fresh and personal manifestation."

THE DOCTRINE OF INSPIRATION MAY BE A POWER
IN THE LIFE OF THE CHURCH.

No divine truth, especially a truth on which rests
the authority and power of a book, the teachings of
which are so knit into the very fabric of human life,
can be without its direct, practical bearing. Something
is wrong when such a truth remains only a formula of
the schools. And therefore the question is pertinent
why the truth of inspiration, in itself considered,
should not exert a divine virtue and be a living factor
of spiritual life and energy in the church? A correct
conception of the character and meaning of Biblical inspiration ought to vindicate for itself an inspiring
power. "The real test of all inspiration," as the author just quoted remarks, "lies in the measure of its
ability to inspire," and such ability ought to lie in its
conception as well as in its operation. Such a conception is not impossible for the average mind. If the
personal Christ can be apprehended, so also can the in-

spiration of Scripture as an expression of his divine and human personality. If the fact and the quality of inspiration be identified with a personal power and a personal testimony in Scripture, if men be taught to discern in Scripture a divine witness to faith and love and holiness gathering itself from every part into the perfect manhood of Jesus—then the doctrine of inspiration can be taught, not only so as to appeal to the average intelligence, but also with power to kindle the spiritual consciousness and to evoke its sympathetic response. If the ear of this age could be opened to that voice of the God-man filled with the Holy Ghost and speaking in Scripture, if its heart could be laid bare to that testimony, the attitude of the apostolic age toward Scripture would be reproduced. Earlier conditions, it is true, are not better because they are earlier; but it is certain that Scripture appealed to the apostolic church as a whole with a freshness, a vividness, a simplicity, a directness, and a power of conviction which are too much wanting in the modern church. The reason was that Scripture was searched chiefly in order to hear in it the voice and the testimony of Jesus.

If we are content to drop out of the current of this majestic movement of Christ in Scripture, and to busy ourselves with the explanation of an eddy or a backset here and there, we are out of the current of inspiration, and in contact with something which has no more power of inspiration than a stone. What the world needs in the Bible is not the demonstration that Moses wrote the whole Pentateuch or that Isaiah is the work of a single author: not the mathematical precision of Euclid, nor the doctrinal systematizing of Calvin, but the testimony of the living Christ; the history of God in Christ reconciling the world unto himself; the spiritual impact of men moved by the Spirit of Christ; the mighty influence of that whole mass of history, psalmody, proverb, prophecy, biography, gospel and epistle, witnessing in human souls to the authority of the unseen, and vindicating the claims of eternity against those of time and sense. The Bible means to the Church this or nothing. A book that will meet this demand, and thus show itself profitable for teaching, for reproof, for correction, for discipline, for perfecting a man of God, can easily carry all the verbal errors and discrepancies of number and date which may attach to it. They are like flies on the panoply of a giant. The Bible is a means, not an end. The design of revelation does not culminate in a book, but in Christ. The book is less than Christ, though Christ is its central theme and its inspiration. If we choose to devote our energy to the utterly hopeless effort to vindicate inspiration on the basis of the letter, we shall get out of touch with the spiritual potency and divine magnetism of the Bible, and shall dwarf the Bible in our own conception. To no purpose is it that the bush burns with fire and sends forth a divine voice, so long as we are intent only on the relation and arrangement of the twigs, or engrossed in watching whether each tongue of flame issues at the same angle with every other.

[A large part of this pamphlet was published in the *New World* of March, 1893, and is reprinted here with the permission of the editors.]